WITHDRAWN

_________ SOUTH SCHOOL

on the water

SOUTH SCHOOL

5
6

on the water

by E. and R. S. Radlauer

illustrated with photographs by the authors

E. S. E. A.
TITLE II

Franklin Watts, Inc., 845 Third Avenue, New York, N.Y. 10022
Library of Congress Cataloging in Publication Data on page 48.
Copyright © 1973 by E. and R. S. Radlauer
Printed in the United States of America.
5   4   3   2   1

SOUTH SCHOOL

A lot of us have been around the water for years and years. We spend our time fishing and watching. Fishing is important for those who need it to make a living. During the time that we're not out fishing we like to watch some of the strange things that happen on the water. Some are very strange, I'll say. Just when I think I've seen it all, something else shows up. At first I think each new sport is greater than the old ones. Then when I go back and see some of the old sports, I can see how they were pretty good, too.

Just being old doesn't mean that something isn't good anymore. After all, as far as I can tell, the ocean is very old. The age of the ocean doesn't seem to stop people from using it—right?

4

Come on in! The watching is great if you like to watch what happens on the water.

The idea of standing or walking on water is a little unusual, I'd say. Of course, swimming is different. We've been doing that for years and years. But standing up on the water is something else. Or maybe I should say I see lots of people trying to stand up on the water. It's called **surfing**. Some of it's good, some of it isn't so good. If someone stays on a **surfboard**, that's good. Falling off, well, that's not so good. The idea is to keep the board just in front of the breaking wave. As the wave breaks, the rider rolls along with the surf. When a surfer falls off his board he gets to practice his swimming.

The way a surfer matches the speed of the board to the speed of the wave is part of the balance. To match the speed of the board to the wave, the surfer changes his body balance. The front to rear balance is what holds the board in the wave. That's only one thing a surfer has to practice. Next, he has to practice side to side balance and how to steer. Besides all the balancing, a surfer has to watch where the board is going. When someone is out there surfing, he'd better think about what he's doing and nothing else.

I've even heard that someone on a surf-*board* doesn't have time to feel *bored* at all. My mother didn't think that was funny, either. She says my jokes are for the birds. I wonder what she means by that.

Surfing takes plenty of watching. Especially if
you're the one doing the surfing.

When someone wipes out on a surfboard it's
time to go swimming.

SOUTH SCHOOL

Except for going on the water, **drag boats** aren't very much like surfboards. At 200 miles per hour drag boats make their own waves. I guess a speed like that makes them the fastest things on the water—almost like flying. Well, not really flying, but 200 miles per hour is hauling, on the water or anywhere else. The boats have engines that turn out over a thousand **horsepower**. Some of the boats have special equipment like wings or tails to help them go straight. That always seemed funny to me, putting wings or tails on a boat. I always thought that wings and tails were standard equipment for flying. But it takes plenty of equipment to keep a boat moving 200 miles an hour going in the right direction. Going the wrong way, like down, could mean trouble.

At 200 miles an hour, a drag boat makes a pretty good surf.

Red Baron
65

It's OK for drag boats to go up, as long as it's not too far up. For a boat to get up a real good speed, there shouldn't be much of it in the water. The water drags on the boat, slows it down. That's not where drag boat racing got its name, but it's true, anyway. To go very fast a boat has to lift up and sort of skim over the water. That's why boats may have **fins** on the bottom. The fins are supposed to keep the boat going straight while the bottom goes through the water. Well, that's how it's supposed to work. Most of the time it works OK. Now and then something doesn't work the way it's supposed to work.

When things don't go the way they're supposed to, it's called trouble. Sometimes there's big trouble and at other times it may be little trouble. I think that when a boat is cut in half, it's big trouble. It can happen when someone in a boat race makes a turn. Now there isn't anything wrong with making a turn, but if it happens right in front of another boat, then there is something wrong. It means the kind of trouble where a boat ends up in two pieces, cut in half. This time no one was hurt. The half of the boat with nothing in it, the back half, went to the bottom. The other half, the piece with the engine in it, didn't sink. With all that trouble the owner was glad he didn't have to fish for his engine. Did someone say "fish"?

When a drag boat tries to fly like a bird, there's something to watch. Is this driver trying to keep his boat dry?

If, after a race, you end up with half a boat, it's better than no boat at all.

SOUTH SCHOOL

I guess it's because of the speed that boat racing has so many safety rules. One important rule is about **life jackets**. If someone goes into the water the jacket or **life vest** is to keep him from drowning. Another safety rule says that anyone in a very fast boat must wear a **helmet**. The helmet should hook under the driver's arms, onto his life vest. If someone hit the water at 150 miles per hour, a helmet would be like a water parachute. A water parachute strapped to a driver's chin could give him a very hard pull on his neck. That's why the helmet hooks onto the life vest. Long necks look good on swans, not drag boat drivers.

A drag boat has to be built right, according to the safety rules. At 200 miles per hour the engine and other parts must turn some pretty high **revolutions per minute**, or **RPM's**. If a part breaks when it's turning a high RPM, it doesn't just break, it explodes. Pieces of metal flying out of a **gearbox** or **drive shaft** are not exactly good for a boat or driver. Flying parts might be bad. A **scattershield** is supposed to keep pieces of metal from exploding out of a broken drive shaft or gearbox. According to the rules, the scattershield must be of an exact thickness and placed around any part that might explode and finish off a boat—or driver.

All powerboat racers should wear a life vest and
helmet. It helps if they know how to swim, too.

A scattershield covers shafts and gearboxes.
That's good for safety. So is the fire extinguisher.

When a boat has the engine or engines outside, there isn't so much danger from moving parts. Maybe that's why some people like **outboards**, boats with the engines outside. When the engine is outside there's more room inside. On an outboard there's even a place for dark windows that keep the driver from getting too much sunshine. No telling what the driver is doing in there. He might even be cooking up some fish chowder. Oh, boy, who said fish chowder? That's great stuff for drivers who are inboard, outboard, overboard, or just plain bored with hamburgers and french fries. Let's all hang around the water thinking about fish chowder instead of hamburgers and french fries.

14

With the engines outboard, there's plenty of room inboard. Anybody home?

Tipster
Carlson
CHRYSLER
61
61
GARY FERGUSON

This could be the one boat that can make me forget about fish chowder. In the "wild looks" department the Bat Boat has to be the winner. Besides being different in the "wild looks" department, the Bat Boat has a different kind of power drive, a **jet pump** instead of a **propeller**. Most boats use a propeller to push them through the water. A **jet boat,** like the Bat Boat, uses a pump that gulps in water and then pushes it out the back. It sort of pumps itself through the water. Jet boats aren't faster or slower than propeller-style boats but some people like them because they're safer. They're safer in case the driver runs over someone in the water. A turning propeller could do some damage to a person—or a fish, even.

It's a bird! It's a boat! It's Bat Boat.

When a drag boat starts off, there's more to hear than quiet. The roar might scatter everything for miles around. Of course, some of us are used to the roaring. We stay to watch, because there's plenty to see when the driver puts on the power, maybe 1,000 horsepower worth. A boat needs that kind of power to move it on the water at 200 miles per hour. At that speed a boat may cover the quarter-mile **drag course** in about seven or eight seconds. As a boat goes faster, the **rooster tail**, the spray of water, gets higher and longer. If a driver doesn't want a shower, he'd better be out front. Following a fast drag boat is probably a sure way to get a bath.

So now we find out that anyone wanting a shower bath can get it by following a very fast boat. That's something to see—a giant rooster tail that flies 50 feet up in the air. But anyone wanting to use this kind of a shower bath has to go fast. The shower moves over the water at 200 miles per hour and only lasts for a few seconds. That hardly leaves time for soap. Lots of people put out a birdbath and let the bird make his own shower. I guess a rooster tail shower that goes fast would be for some kind of a drag bird, whatever that is.

You can really tell when a drag boat starts to move out. The rooster tail starts to grow

. . . and grow until there's more rooster tail than drag boat.

Sometimes 1,000 horsepower and a 200-mile-per-hour speed can't win a race. That happens when the engine quits and leaves the boat dead in the water. For a drag boat driver that's bad news. Now it's time to finish the race the hard way. There's only one way to finish a race with a dead engine. Row, row, row your boat. Keep on rowing until the boat crosses the finish line. The driver wants to finish the race so he won't be **disqualified,** out of the day's racing. Finishing a race at a speed of two miles per hour is better than being disqualified. So here we are, using manpower in place of horsepower.

Lifeguards have to be more than good at rowing, they have to be expert. They'd better be expert if they want to save someone who is drowning. So once a year the lifeguards get together to have a rowing contest. Part of the contest is to see which team is best at rowing through the surf. After all, if someone were out in the surf drowning and yelling for help, the lifeguard team should be able to row out and save him. It wouldn't be good if all the lifeguards could do was yell back at the drowning guy and say, "Sorry, we don't know how to row. Come back some other day." The contest shows which lifeguards are expert and which ones need to be more expert at rowing.

Did anyone ever raise a rooster tail while rowing a boat?

When rowing through surf, remember to head straight into the wave.

Of course, if someone were out swimming and was about to drown, he might not have time to pick the expert team to save him. He wouldn't be part of a contest. But during the rowing contest even expert teams had trouble because their boats got into arguments. Going through surf in a boat is hard enough without making it part of a race. From far away the surf may look smooth. Close up though, it's rough. That's when the boats start to tangle or argue with each other. It looks as if one boat is going up. Is the other going to go down? I think I'll stick around and find out how a boat argument ends.

Now we get to see how it is when lifeguard rowboats get into a tangle. The boat that loses the argument is sitting in the water, upside down. Or is it downside up? The lifeguards are sitting in the water trying to figure out what happened. Maybe they're trying to figure out what to do next. Let's see, shall we swim for shore? Shall we head for China? No, China's too far away for swimming. Or should we try to get our boat right side up? They'd better hurry up or we'll be sending out some lifeguards to fish some lifeguards out of the water. Did someone say "fish"? Great, maybe we'll have a lifeguard fishing contest. Or should it be a contest fishing for lifeguards?

If you don't head straight into the wave you may go right, left, up, or down.

Do we need a lifeguard to go rescue the lifeguards?

Besides the lifeguard contest we have other rowing competition on the water. **Crew racing** is probably the fastest rowing competition there is. It got its name because each boat has a bunch of rowers called a crew. The boats aren't called boats, either. They're called **shells**. The shell is very lightweight and made just for racing. The crew sits in the shell and gets ready to race. There may be four, six, or eight people on the crew to do the rowing. There's a person called the **coxswain** who sits in the back and does the steering. The coxswain wears a thing on his mouth that looks like a bird's beak, you might say. You might say—I wouldn't.

When the crew race begins, everyone on the crew has to row hard. But each rower can't row any old way he wants. That's where the coxswain, the guy with the beak, the **megaphone,** comes in. He uses the megaphone to yell at the people on the crew. No, he's not telling them jokes. He's telling them how to row, how fast, which side should pull harder, and stuff like that. Besides yelling, the person with the megaphone has to steer the boat. The rowers are riding backward, pulling and hoping to get to the finish line without running into another boat. They have to trust the person steering and hope he knows where to go.

There aren't any waves in a crew race, just plenty of rowing.

The person in the back says, "Hey, crew, it helps if everyone rows together."

SOUTH SCHOOL

Is this any place for a rowboat, out in the rough **white water** of a river? Well, it's probably no place for a crew in a shell, but it's a pretty good place for someone in an air-filled plastic **torpedo boat**. The torpedo boat got its name because it's shaped like one, a torpedo. It's made of strong plastic that stays afloat as long as it's filled with air. A torpedo boat rider has to follow the flow of the river and use the oar to keep the boat from going into the very rough white water. The rider also uses the oar to keep the boat away from sharp rocks that might do a little damage to the plastic. Or I might say big damage. Looks easy, doesn't it?

Who said you couldn't go surfing in the river?
Well, it's almost like surfing while sitting down.

Some things look easy until they stop being easy. That's what happens when a torpedo boat gets into rough water. It's almost like surfing on the river, a kind of **wipe out** time. The boat folds in the middle and looks like a big bird getting ready to fly. Maybe it's time for the riders to get out and head for shore. Most people don't try to ride the very rough water. They just ride their boat in the calm water, staying away from the rough stuff. If someone likes to row a while and maybe just ride with the river a while, the torpedo boat is a pretty good idea. We'll just wish these riders better luck next time.

28

It is like surfing when someone wipes out. It's time to go swimming.

Some people don't want to row any of the time. They'd rather take a VW car for a drive on the water. So there it is, a **raft** powered by a VW car. I guess it's a good idea as long as they stay away from the white water. A low-powered VW engine won't give the raft any drag boat speed, but on such a beautiful day who wants speed anyway? All these guys have to do is keep the engine running, enjoy the beautiful day, and watch where they're going. What would happen if the raft got into some white water and started to fold up? Of course, the VW is waterproof. Or it's supposed to be waterproof. Maybe the raft crew would be able to drive the VW on the water.

A VW raft beats surfing, rowing, or swimming.

There is one kind of car or vehicle that people can drive on the water. It's the **all terrain vehicle**, the **ATV**, good for driving on water, sand, rocks, hills, almost anywhere. Small fins on the fat tires move the vehicle through the water. Because it's very light, the ATV can get along with a small engine. The driver steers by changing the speed of the wheels on each side of the vehicle. While it's on the water, the ATV isn't anything special in the speed department. But for those who like to get around riding on six wheels, the ATV is a pretty good machine. To get more speed, some people ride another kind of ATV, one that has two wheels instead of six.

I guess the motorcycle is a kind of all terrain vehicle, too. It wasn't built for running in water, but it happens all the time. It happens when there's a water crossing in a motorcycle **Moto Cross race**. Some riders may slow down for the water crossing while others hit it like drag boat drivers. After a few hours of racing, the water crossing gets a little muddy and very slippery. The thing gets to be a kind of *Mudo* Cross instead of Moto Cross. As the race day goes on, there are fewer and fewer riders left in the running. A drowned-out engine never finished a race. Maybe these riders should put wings on their machines. Then they could fly over the water without getting wet.

It's a boat! It's a car! It's a dune buggy. It's really a boat-car-dune-buggy called an All Terrain Vehicle or ATV.

Everybody wants to be on the water, even Moto Cross riders. Or is this Mudo Cross racing?

Now and then there's something in, on, or around the water that isn't so great. It's garbage, trash, or **pollution**. That pollution stuff is real bad news. Does anyone want to go surfing on garbage? How about a drag boat race through some trash? And wouldn't it be fun to row a boat through a bunch of pollution. There isn't much anyone can do in water that's dirty and polluted. But just think of what that polluted water does to the fish! I can't stand to think about that. Maybe we should all think about ways to clean up our water or there won't be any of us left to use it for fishing, sports, or anything else.

34

Pollution on the water is bad, no matter where it happens.

If the water is clean, we may see a person going down into the water to visit the fish. Only the way this **diver** is dressed, in a diver's outfit, he isn't going to be able to say much to the fish. The outfit has a **hard hat helmet**, weights to make the diver sink, and hoses for breathing. Fish don't need hoses for breathing—they take their oxygen right out of the water, if it isn't polluted. A diver needs a breathing mixture of oxygen and helium. The special mixture keeps the diver from getting sick and dizzy. Without the mixture of oxygen and helium the diver couldn't go very deep or stay down very long.

While the diver is under the water, like maybe 250 feet down, he can work on all kinds of things. He can make lots of bubbles, that's for sure. While he's making bubbles he may be working on something that drills holes to find out what's in the ground, under the water. He may be looking for a wrecked boat. He may be working on something that will hold a bridge, or he may just be looking around to see what he can find. Sometimes there's gold or jewelry in a wrecked boat. I guess for those that like it, being underwater looking for jewelry is great. But there are others who don't want to be in, on, or under the water.

A diver likes to see what's in and under the water. It looks like time to visit a fish.

At 250 feet down, a diver can do more than make bubbles. He usually has lots of work to do.

A kite flyer wants to be off the water. But the ride has to start on the water. The kite flyer uses water skis while being towed by a fast boat. As the boat picks up speed, the flyer rides the rooster tail. When the boat hits 45 miles per hour or so, the flyer goes **airborne**, off the water and about 50 feet up in the air. It takes plenty of muscles to hold the kite, hang on, stay airborne, and not drop the water skis. Any kind of flying takes muscles, I'll say. Kite flying looks like fun, but I think it's a hard way to fly. Still, for someone without wings, it's probably as good a way as any.

As long as the boat keeps up speed, the kite flyer is OK. The faster the boat goes, the higher the ride. Of course the ride isn't any higher than the length of the **towrope**. There are even some kinds of kites where the flyer can cut loose from the rope and sail like a bird. Then the length of the towrope doesn't make any difference. But in the towrope kind of flying, the rider just sails along, watching the water, the boat, and the rooster tail. As long as there's a big rooster tail, the flying is great. If the rooster tail drops because the boat stops, the kite flyer drops, too. He makes one quick landing, kite, skis, and all.

A kite flyer likes to be on the water, but only for a while.

What a kite flyer really likes to do is be up, off the water. Is it time to visit the birds?

SOUTH SCHOOL

There's no telling what else is going to happen out here, on the water. Mostly it's all pretty
great. I like to watch the kite flyers, the rowers,
even the bubbles from the divers. The great-
est, I think, is the rooster tail that follows the
drag boats. Of course the pollution stuff is
very bad news. That hurts everybody and if
we don't watch it, all the water sports and the
fishing are going to end. Oh, yes, there's one
more thing that I don't like. It's a certain kind
of sign that I see once in a while. Anyone that
does fishing doesn't like that kind of sign, I'm
sure.

*Kite flyers, drag boats, divers, surfers, rowboats
—what next?*

Now here's that certain kind of sign that I don't like. Just who do they think they are, putting up a sign like that, telling me NO FISH-ING. Did I ever put up a sign that said NO SURFING or NO ROWING or NO BOAT RAC-ING? I wonder if someday I might even see a sign that says NO FLYING. That sign must be for someone else. I'll just forget about it. A sign like that just *isn't* for the birds.

42

Anybody that puts up a NO FISHING sign better watch out. Besides, what makes them think I can read, anyway?

NO FISHING

Glossary/Index

(Page number indicates where
the word first appears in the book)

On a boat, the box that holds the boat's drive gears. These are forward, reverse, and neutral (stop).

A helmet that holds the driver's breathing supply and protects his head.

A hard padded hat to protect the head.

The power needed to lift 33,000 pounds one foot for one minute equals one horsepower.

A jet boat uses a jet or pump to move itself through the water.

What people wear to keep them afloat when they fall in the water.

A cone used for sending the voice in a certain direction.

A dirt track motorcycle race that has steep hills, jumps, sharp turns, and sometimes a water crossing.

Outside of the boat.

Garbage, trash, or any material that makes water (or air or land) unfit.

A part of a boat's motor that turns and pushes the boat through the water.

Raft, p. 30
A floating platform.

Revolutions per minute, RPM, p. 12
How fast something is turning. One RPM means one turn or revolution per minute.

Rooster tail, p. 18
The spray of water sent up by a fast boat.

Scattershield, p. 12
A metal covering or special blanket to keep broken parts from flying out of a broken driveshaft or gearbox.

Shell, p. 24
A long thin rowboat made of light wood or plastic, used in crew competition.

Surfboard, p. 6
A plastic board used for riding on waves.

Surfing, p. 6
Riding on a wave by using a plastic board.

Torpedo boat, p. 26
A long thin inflated plastic boat with a sharp nose.

Towrope, p. 38
A rope used to pull another boat.

White water, p. 26
Water that is moving so fast that the foam on it makes it look white.

Wipe out, p. 28
To lose control of, upset, or fall out of a boat. Also, to fall off a surfboard.

About the Authors

Ruth and Ed Radlauer, authors of over sixty books for young people, are graduates of UCLA. They have worked as teachers, school administrators, reading specialists, and instructors in creative writing. Their works include books in the areas of science, language, social studies, and, more recently, high-interest reading materials. Their other Sports Action books published by Franklin Watts are *Buggy-Go-Round, Scramble Cycle, On the Drag Strip, On the Sand, Horsing Around, Chopper Cycle,* and *Salt Cycle.*

Along with their three children, two horses, two motorcycles, a dog, and an ancient cat, the Radlauers live in La Habra, California.

PHOTO CREDITS
Pages 27 and 29, *Orange Torpedo Trips,* Grants Pass, Oregon
Page 31, *Ernie Ziehm,* Whittier, California
Page 37, *Oceaneering International,* Santa Barbara, California

Library of Congress Cataloging in Publication Data

Radlauer, Edward.
    On the water.

    (Sports action books)
    SUMMARY: Briefly describes such diversified water sports as surfing, drag boat racing, diving, and rafting.
    1. Aquatic sports—Juvenile literature.
[1. Aquatic sports] I. Radlauer, Ruth Shaw, joint author. II. Title.
GV775.R34   797   72-7085
ISBN 0-531-02586-1